for Marjorie
from Dorothea
with love
July 1990

A Flight of Cranes

A Flight of Cranes:

stories and poems from around the world about cranes

Compiled and edited with notes by
DOROTHEA HAYWARD SCOTT

A Flight of Cranes: Stories and Poems from Around the World.
ISBN 0 9516075 0 2

First published 1990 by
The Denvil Press

Typeset and printed by smallprint
35 Silver Birches, Haywards Heath, West Sussex RH16 3PD

For Kate and Carlos Iber

and their mother

Martha Johnson

who introduced me to the cranes at Baraboo

Contents

The illustrations on pages x, 12, 17, 18, 26 and 46 are from *Cranes of the World* by Paul A. Johnsgard (1983) and are reproduced by courtesy of Indiana University Press, Bloomington, U.S.A. Those on pages 24 and 44 are from a *Coloring Book of Cranes* drawn by Sue Rogers (1981) and are reproduced by courtesy of the International Crane Foundation.

Foreword

Cranes are enormous and stunningly beautiful birds. Everything they do seems deliberate and graceful. They dance when content or courting. They communicate with both subtle posturing and low purr-like calls as well as with brazen strutting and trumpet-like cries that carry for several miles. They can travel thousands of miles at astounding altitudes. Cranes are monogamous. Well-mated pairs act like a single unit and they lavish attention on their chicks. Clearly there are many parallels between cranes and humans. We stand about the same height, we also both have intricate communication. Men are apparently monogamous with highly developed parental care.

It is not unusual then that since times untold, people of many cultures have not only appreciated the remarkable aesthetic appeal of cranes, but they have personified cranes in folklore, featuring them as both moral and supernatural entities. Cranes were given those qualities for which humans strive.

Hisako, a victim of the atomic bombing of Hiroshima, believed that if she made 1,000 origami cranes she would be healed. Although she died before meeting her objective, today the crane is a symbol of peace. Recently, cranes have been vehicles for international cooperation as men from many nations now co-operate to save these ancient birds from extinction.

Dorothea Scott has brought together from many cultures a compilation of stories and poems whose unifying element is the crane. Her excellent collection of classical literature, followed by a brief account of crane biology, blend to provide the reader a fuller understanding of the real and imagined qualities of these extraordinary birds.

George Archibald, *Director*
International Crane Foundation

Introduction

Cranes have been on Earth for longer than almost any other living creature. Fossil records of cranes date back millions of years. No wonder they have featured in so many stories and legends from around the world. A sad fact is that cranes were far more numerous than they are now and were familiar to many more people. As their natural habitats of swamps and marshlands have been drained or otherwise destroyed they have retreated to remoter regions to nest and breed in the Spring and to special refuges to winter where abundant food is provided.

Here are stories from native Americans of Indiana and Canada, from Blacks in Kenya and from Aboriginals in Australia. Fables from Aesop are included, as also are quaint stories and poems translated from ancient Greek and Latin which were collected by an English naturalist, Edward Topsell, in the seventeenth century. Other early Latin references show that cranes were known in the past in the British Isles and they were included by Chaucer in his listing of familiar birds. Some of the oldest stories and poems come from China and Japan where the crane is held in special veneration. In these fables, stories and poems cranes are clever, resourceful and affectionate, but it is their proud grace and beauty which makes them so beloved.

Common Crane

Fables, Stories and Poems from Classical Times and from Medieval and Renaissance Europe

Among the oldest and most widespread of stories about birds and animals are the fables of Aesop retold in every language. Most of the fables have no extant early texts (they were passed down orally) but have been translated, edited and added to from early Greek, Latin and Indian language collections of stories. Aesop himself is traditionally believed to have been an educated Phrygian slave who gained his freedom among his Greek masters by his gift for wittily introducing fables in telling arguments with them.

The crane is shown as clever in getting its own back on the fox, kind in helping even a dangerous wolf in difficulties, and noble in scorning the vanity of a peacock.

The Fox and the Crane

A fox invited a crane to dinner, and served soup in a very shallow dish. The crane was unable to eat it and the fox laughed. Returning the invitation, the crane served the meal in a tall, narrow jar. The fox couldn't get his head into the jar and went home hungry.

Moral: Different people do different things well.

This fable and the following one are taken from *Aesop's Fables Coloring Book.* Used by courtesy of Dover Publications Inc., ©1972. The illustrations are enlarged from woodcuts in one of the earliest printed editions made in Ulm, Germany, in 1476.

The Wolf and the Crane

A wolf once got a bone stuck in his throat. He offered money to a crane if she would put her head into his mouth and pull the bone out of his throat. She did what he wanted and asked for her money. The wolf, laughing and baring his teeth, said, "Forget about the money. Just be glad that you got your head out of a wolf's mouth safe and sound."

Moral: If you deal with nasty people, don't expect too much.

The Peacock and the Crane

The peacock and the crane having by chance met together, the peacock erected his tail, displayed his gaudy plumes, and looked with contempt upon the crane, as some mean ordinary person. The crane, resolving to mortify his insolence, took occasion to say that peacocks were very fine birds indeed, if fine feathers could make them so; but that he thought that it a much nobler thing to be able to rise above the clouds into endless space, and survey the wonders of the heavens, as well as of the earth beneath, with its seas, lakes, and rivers, as far as the eyes can reach, than to strut about upon the ground, and be gazed at by children.

Application: There cannot be a greater sign of a weak mind, than a person's valuing himself on a gaudy outside . . . .

From *The Fables of Aesop and Others with Designs on Wood* by Thomas Bewick. Newcastle, England, 1818.

Cranes were common in Europe in earlier times although now found only in Scandinavian countries. A charming story is told by Saint Columba who lived from AD 521-597. He was born in Ireland where he is venerated for his work in founding monastic schools. He sailed to Scotland with some followers, landed on Iona and founded a monastery there. Before he died the whole of Scotland became Christian.

St. Columba and the Crane

And another time it befell, while the Saint was living on Iona, that he called one of the brethren to him, to speak to him. "Go thou", he said, "three days from now to the west of this island at dawn, and sit above the shore and wait: for when the third hour before sunset is past, there shall come flying from the northern coast of Ireland a stranger guest, a crane, wind tossed and driven far from her course in the high air: tired out and weary she will fall on the beach at thy feet and lie there, her strength nigh gone: tenderly lift her and carry her to the steading near by: make her welcome there and cherish her with all care for three days and nights; and when the three days are ended, refreshed and loath to tarry longer with us in our exile, she shall take flight again towards that old sweet land of Ireland whence she came, in pride of strength once more: and if I commend her so earnestly to thy charge, it is that in that countryside where thou and I were reared, she too was nested."

The brother obeyed: and on the third day, when the third hour before sunset was past, stood as he was bidden, in wait for the coming of the promised guest: and when she had come and lay fallen on the beach, he lifted her and carried her ailing to the steading, and fed her, famished as she was. And on his return that evening to the monastery the Saint spoke to him, not as one questioning but as one speaks of a thing past. "May God bless thee, my son", said he, "for thy kind tending of this pilgrim guest: that shall make no long stay in her exile, but when three suns have set shall turn back to her own land."

And the thing fell out even as the Saint had foretold. For when her three days housing was ended, and as her host stood by, she rose in first flight from the earth into high heaven, and after a while at gaze to spy out her aerial way, took her straight flight above the quiet sea, and so to Ireland through the tranquil weather.

From *Beasts and Saints:* Translations (from original Latin texts) by Helen Waddell. London, Constable, 1934.

"The Parliament of Fowls"

Chaucer, in a long poem called *The Parliament of Fowls,* composed about 1382 probably in celebration of a royal marriage, imagines that on Saint Valentine's Day a gathering of birds, presided over by the Goddess of nature, meets to choose their mates. The crane is naturally among their number.

. . . There was the dove, with her eyes meek
The jealous swan, ayens his death that singeth,
The owl eke, that of death the bode bringeth.
The crane, the giant, with his trumpet sound;
The thief, the chough, and eke the jangling pye;
The scorning jay; the eel's foe, the heron,
The false lapwing, full of treachery . . .

From *The Complete Works of Geoffrey Chaucer.* Edited from numerous manuscripts by Walter W. Skeat. London, Oxford University Press, Humphrey Milford, 1927. (The spelling has been modernised by the editor.)

"The Fowles of Heaven or a History of Birdes"

Early in the seventeenth century Edward Topsell wrote a book, *The Fowles of Heaven or a History of Birdes* with a chapter on the 'Crane'. Besides the most accurate description of cranes he could gather from information available in his day, he collected stories, poems and observations about cranes from ancient Greek and Roman writers as well as some poems by Renaissance writers nearer his own time. In this chapter we find:

> . . . The other thing observed in their flight is the form and fashion wherein they rank themselves, for while the air is calm and not troubled with boisterous winds, they fly triangularly like the Greek letter *lambda*, pointed before and forked behind, that so before them the air may be cut and pierced more easily, but behind them, the open passage foremost and hindmost may be benefited by the blast thereof.
>
> . . . they change places in their course . . . every one in his order, after a certain distance of time and place.

He then quotes poems about the flight and migration of cranes:

When cranes do leave their summer dwelling, Thrace,
And change Strymona with the warmer river Nile:
With wings they write plain letters, varying place,
Scribbling in air with quills uncut and wild.

This poem was written by the last of the great poets of ancient Rome, Claudius Claudianus (AD 305-404). The one which follows was written by Lodovico Ariosto (1474-1543) who was famous for writing a great romantic epic, *Orlando Furioso.*

As we see strange cranes are wont to do
First stalk a while ere they their wings can find
Then soar from ground not past a yard or two,
Till in their wings they gathered have the wind;
At last they mount the very clouds unto
Trianglewise according to their kind.

Then comes a couplet written in Latin about the migration of cranes in the Spring by a poet-monk known as Mantuan from the place where he was born in 1448:

When cranes come hither tis Spring and sowing time.
They feed on grain uncovered which they find.

Edward Topsell finally translates this story from the Latin of Gregorius Nyssenius who retold it from classical Greek and follows it by quoting an epigram based on the story by Sidonius Apollinaris who lived about AD 430-483:

The Avengers of Ibycus

The lyric poet, Ibycus, was walking alone on a country road when a band of robbers set upon him mortally wounding him. As he lay dying a flight of cranes passed overhead, so he called out to them, "Bear witness to this deed!" No one could discover how Ibycus met his death.

Later that year the same band of robbers was mingling with the crowd in the Corinth market place. When a flight of cranes passed overhead, one of the robbers said to the other without thinking, "There go the avengers of the death of Ibycus!" He was overheard and the group were summoned for questioning. Eventually they admitted their guilt and paid the price for their wicked deed.

When robbers once to deserts came,
O Ibycus thy blood to spill:
thou didst beseech a cloud of cranes
To witness their accursed will.
And not in vain; the Furies brought
Revenge on them in Corinth land . . .

Ever afterwards if a mystery was solved by some strange means, people would remark, "Ah, the cranes of Ibycus!"

From *The Fowles of Heaven or History of Birdes* by Edward Topsell; Chapter XXXIII, 'Crane'. (The spelling has been modernised in the passages quoted, which are taken from the University of Texas 1972 edition, edited by T. P. Harrison and F. D. Hoeniger.)

Stories from Africa and Australia

Crowned Crane

The beautiful crowned cranes are found only in Africa so that it is natural to have a story from there to account for this distinctive headdress.

Crane dances have been associated with several ancient cultures but such dances can still be seen in ceremonies among the aboriginal tribes in Australia.

Arap Sang and the Cranes
(How Cranes got their Crowns)

A gift is a great responsibility to the giver, people of Africa say, and after they have said that they may tell you the story of Arap Sang and the Cranes.

Arap Sang was a great chief and more than half a god, for in the days when he lived great chiefs were always a little mixed up with the gods. One day he was walking on the plain admiring the cattle. It was hot. The rains had not yet come; the ground was almost bare of grass and as hard as stone; the thorn trees gave no shade for they were just made of long spines and thin twigs and tiny leaves and the sun went straight through them. It was hot. Only the black ants didn't feel it and they would be happy in a furnace.

Arap Sang was getting old and the sun beat down on his bald head and he thought: "I'm feeling things more than I used to." And then he came across a vulture sitting in the crotch of a tree, his wings hanging down and his eyes on the lookout.

"Vulture," said Arap Sang, "I'm hot and the sun is making my head ache. You have there a fine pair of broad wings. I'd be most grateful if you'd spread them out and let an old man enjoy a patch of shade."

"Why?" croaked Vulture.

"Because it wouldn't be much trouble to you. Because it's pleasant and good to help people."

"Bah!" said Vulture.

"What's that?"

"Oh, go home, Baldy, and stop bothering people; it's hot."

Arap Sang straightened himself up and his eyes flashed. He wasn't half a god for nothing and when he was angry he could be rather a terrible old person. And he was very angry now. The really terrifying thing was that when he spoke he didn't shout. He spoke quietly and the words were clear and cold and hard and all separate like hailstones.

"Vulture," he said, "you're cruel and you're selfish. I shan't forget what you've said and you won't either. NOW GET OUT!" Arap Sang was so impressive that Vulture got up awkwardly and flapped off.

Arap Sang walked on. He was feeling shaky. And he did want a bit of shade. Presently he met an elephant. Elephant was panting across the plain in a tearing hurry and was most reluctant to stop when Arap Sang called to him.

"Elephant," said Arap Sang weakly, "I'm tired and I'm dizzy. I want to go to the forest and into a bit of shade but it's a long way."

"It is hot, isn't it?" said Elephant. "I'm off to the forest myself."

"Would you spread out your great ears and let me walk under them?" asked Arap Sang.

"I'm sorry," said Elephant, "but you'd make my journey so slow. I must get to the forest. I've got the most terrible headache."

"Well, I've got a headache too," protested the old man.

"I'm sure," said Elephant, "and no one could be sorrier about that than I am. Is it a very big headache?"

"Very big," said Arap Sang.

"There now," said Elephant. "Consider how big I am compared to you and what the size of my headache must be."

"Oh, all right," sighed Arap Sang.

"I knew you'd see it that way," said Elephant. "It's just what I was saying about you the other day. You can always rely on Arap Sang, I said, to behave reasonably. Well, good-bye and good luck." And he hurried off in the direction of the distant forest and was soon out of sight.

Poor Arap Sang was now feeling very ill indeed. He sat on the ground and he thought to himself: "I can't go another step unless I get some shade and if I don't get some soon I'm done for."

And there he was found by a flock of cranes. They came dancing through the white grass, stamping their long delicate legs so that the insects flew up in alarm and were at once snapped up in the cranes' beaks. They gathered round Arap Sang sitting on the ground and he looked so old and distressed that they hopped up and down with embarrassment, first on one leg then the other. "Korong! Korong!" they called softly and this happens to be their name as well.

"Good birds," whispered Arap Sang, "you must help me. If I don't reach shade soon I'll die. Help me to the forest."

"But, of course," said the cranes, and they spread their great handsome black and white wings to shade him and helped him to his feet, and together, slowly, they all crossed the plain into the trees.

Then Arap Sang sat in the shade of a fine cotton tree and felt very much better. The birds gathered round him and he looked at them and thought that he had never seen more beautiful creatures in the whole world.

"And kind. Kind as well as beautiful," he muttered. "The two don't always go together. I must reward them. I shan't forget your kindness," he said, "and I'll see that no one else does. Now I want each one of you to come here."

Then the cranes came one after another and bowed before him and Arap Sang stretched out his kindly old hand and gently touched each beautiful sleek head. And where he did this a golden crown appeared and after the birds had gravely bowed their thanks they all flew off to the lake, their new crowns glittering in the evening sun. Arap Sang felt quite recovered. He was very pleased with his gift to the cranes.

Two months later a crane dragged himself to the door of Arap Sang's house. It was a pitiful sight, thin with hunger, feathers broken and muddy from hiding in the reeds. Arap Sang exclaimed in pity and horror.

"Great Chief," said the crane, "we beg you to take back your gift. If you don't there'll soon be not one crane left alive for we are hunted day and night for the sake of our golden crowns." Arap Sang listened and nodded his head in sorrow.

"I'm old and I'm foolish," he said, "and I harm my friends. I had forgotten that men were also greedy and selfish and they'll do anything for gold. Let me undo the wrong I have done by giving without thought. I'll make one more magic."

Then he took their golden crowns and in their place he put a wonderful halo of feathers which they have until this day. But they are still called crowned cranes.

Nyanza is a province in Kenya, central Africa, on the eastern shores of Lake Victoria.

Brolga, the Dancing Girl

Brolga was the favourite of everyone in the tribe, for she was not only the merriest among them, but also their best dancer. The other women were content to beat the ground while the men danced, but Brolga must dance; the dances of her own creation as well as those she had seen. Her fame spread and many came to see her. Some also desired her in marriage, but she always rejected them.

An evil magician, Nonega, was most persistent in his attention, until the old men of the tribe told him that, because of his tribal relationship and his unpleasant personality, they would never allow Brolga to become his wife. "If I can't have her," snarled Nonega, she'll never belong to anyone else." For already he had planned to change her from a girl into some creature.

One day, when Brolga was dancing by herself on an open plain near her camp, Nonega, chanting incantations from the centre of a whirlpool in which he was travelling, enveloped the girl in a dense cloud of dust. There was no sign of Brolga after the whirlpool had passed, but standing in her place was a tall, graceful bird, moving its wings in the same manner as the young dancer had moved her arms. When they saw the resemblance everyone called out "Brolga! Brolga!" The bird seemed to understand and, moving towards them, bowed and performed even more intricate dances than before.

From that time onward the aborigines have called that bird Brolga, and they tell their children how the beautiful girl was transformed into the equally beautiful grey bird which still dances on the flood plains of northern Australia.

From *The Dawn of Time: Australian Aboriginal Myths* in Paintings by Ainslie Roberts with text by Charles P. Mountford.

Brolga

Sandhill Crane

Stories from Native Americans

The crane has played an important part in the cultural and religious life of many native American tribes from earliest times. Cranes frequently appear in their art from ancient paintings on stone to modern craft work using crane motifs.

Clan totems can be a representation of a bird, animal, fish or reptile; the crane is prominent among bird totems adopted. Others are the eagle, the gull, the goose and the hawk. For members of the Crane Clan the crane itself and crane feathers used in some festive or religious ceremonies have particular significance.

The names Crane Island, Crane Creek, Crane Lake and Crane Valley occurring in widespread parts of Canada and the United States, show that in the past these birds were familiar visitors where now they are rarely seen. In the following stories the crane takes its accepted place as part of the everyday natural world.

How Crane got his Long Legs

A tale of the Cree

One day long ago Rabbit thought to himself, I should like to ride on the moon. He looked at the full moon as it came up from the edge of the eastern sky. He watched the moon go up in the sky above him and he watched the moon move across the night sky. Rabbit watched the moon until day came and he could not see the moon any longer.

"If I stand on the high hill at the edge of the world," Rabbit said, "I will be able to get hold of the moon when it comes up."

That night Rabbit stood on the high hill. The moon came up slowly. It was so large in the sky that Rabbit reached out to touch it. He stood on his hind legs, and reached for the moon. He stretched his front legs as far as he could to seize hold of the moon. The moon was too far away. It climbed into the sky and Rabbit watched it, but he could not reach it.

"I will get one of the birds to carry me to the moon," Rabbit said and he went to Eagle. "Carry me to the moon, Eagle," Rabbit said, "I want to ride on the moon, but I cannot reach it. I will pay you if you will take me to the moon."

"No," Eagle said, "I cannot carry you to the moon. It is too far. I cannot."

Rabbit went to Hawk. "No," Hawk said, "I have other business to attend to. I cannot carry you to the moon."

Rabbit went to all the great flying birds. The great flying birds would not carry him to the moon. Rabbit went to the small flying birds. The small flying birds laughed. "You are too big for us to carry you to the moon," they said. "The moon is too far from the earth, we cannot carry you to the moon."

Crane heard Rabbit. "I will try to carry you, Rabbit," Crane said. "Hold on to my legs and I will see if I can fly with you to the moon."

Rabbit did as Crane said. Crane rose into the sky. Rabbit was heavy. Crane spread his great wings. It was all that Crane could do to fly with Rabbit. Rabbit looked down at the earth below. It was very small and it was very far away. It was all that Rabbit could do to hold on to Crane, but he did. Crane came to the moon. "Rabbit," Crane said, "I have done it." Rabbit stepped onto the moon. Then he touched Crane's head. The crown of the crane's head became red under Rabbit's hand. "This is my gift," Rabbit said. "From this day you will wear a headdress of red."

So it was. From that day Crane has a red headdress, and his legs are long. They are longer than the legs of other birds. They were stretched from the weight of Rabbit when Crane carried him to the moon. And if you look when the moon is full in the sky, you will see that Rabbit is still riding on the moon.

From *The Long-tailed Bear and Other Indian Legends*, ©1961 by Natalia M. Belting.

Used by courtesy of the publisher, the Bobbs-Merrill Company Inc.

A tale of the Cree Indians who live near James Bay and the Saskatchewan river in Canada.

Why Crane's Feathers are Brown and Otter Doesn't Feel the Cold

There was once a season when Crane laid her egg after all the other cranes were already hatching their young. Crane laid the egg so late that the young crane did not have time to learn to fly before summer was done. Crane spoke to Otter.

"My son is too young to fly South with us. Keep him with you until I return in the Spring."

"I will do it," Otter said, and he took the young crane to live in his den.

One day Otter went hunting. The young crane was alone. Then Osni, that is, Cold, came into the den and took the young crane away.

"You will stay with me," Osni said. "You will do what I tell you to do," and he took the young crane to his lodge. Every day the young crane did what Osni commanded him, and all day and all night the young crane tended the fire and kept it going. He stirred the hot ashes with his bill so that it was blackened by the fire. He fanned the hot coals with his wings so that the feathers were singed brown by the heat.

Spring came. The young crane went out of the lodge when Osni was not looking.

"Mother," the young crane called. "Mother come and find me."

Otter heard the young crane. Otter went up the mountain. He went to the cave of Thunder and Lightning.

"Help me," Otter said. "Help me get the young crane away from Osni."

"We will do it," they said.

"We have come for the young crane," Otter said to Osni.

"He is my grandson," Osni said. "I want him with me."

"He is not your grandson," Otter said. "Give him up."

"No," Osni said.

"Do it," Thunder said.

"Let the young crane go with Otter," Lightning said.

"No," Osni said.

"Well then," Thunder said.

"We shall see," Lightning said.

Thunder struck Osni with his wings. Lightning tore Osni with his claws. Osni, that is, Cold, fell down in front of his lodge.

Crane came. "You have saved my son. I will give you a feast," she said to Thunder and Lightning, and to Otter, she said "I will make you a gift. You will not feel cold in the winter. You will swim, you will run, you will hunt when the cold is great and the snow is deep, but you will not feel the cold because you took care of my son for me."

From *The Long-tailed Bear and Other Indian Legends.* ©1961 by Natalia M. Belting. Used by courtesy of the publisher, the Bobbs-Merrill Company Inc.

A tale told about sandhill cranes by the Assiniboin Indians, a branch of the Dakota, who live in the valleys of the Saskatchewan and Assiniboin rivers in Canada.

Sandhill Crane

Stories from China and Japan

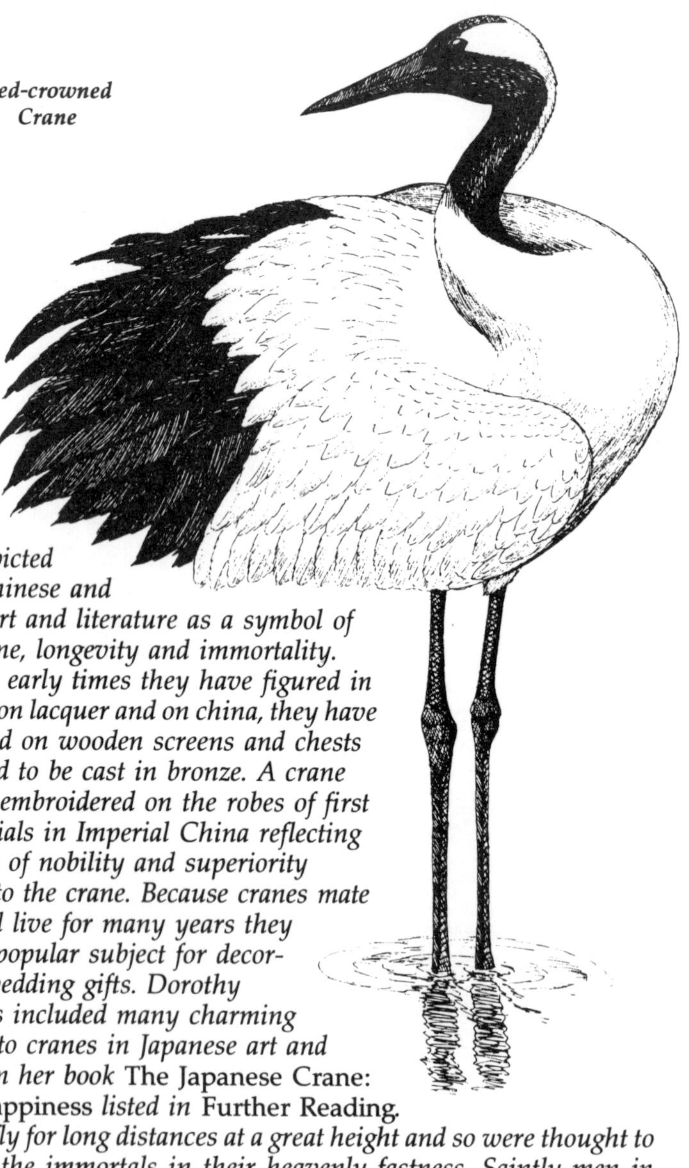

Red-crowned Crane

Cranes have been widely depicted in both Chinese and Japanese art and literature as a symbol of good fortune, longevity and immortality. From very early times they have figured in paintings, on lacquer and on china, they have been carved on wooden screens and chests or modelled to be cast in bronze. A crane motif was embroidered on the robes of first grade officials in Imperial China reflecting the quality of nobility and superiority attributed to the crane. Because cranes mate for life and live for many years they provide a popular subject for decoration on wedding gifts. Dorothy Britton has included many charming references to cranes in Japanese art and literature in her book The Japanese Crane: Bird of Happiness *listed in* Further Reading.

Cranes fly for long distances at a great height and so were thought to be joining the immortals in their heavenly fastness. Saintly men in ancient China withdrew from the world to attain immortality through contemplation. Such sages were often drawn as though travelling to heaven seated on the back of a crane. Alternatively a sage was shown as transformed into a crane himself and so attaining the heavenly regions.

The crane was one of the emblems associated with the literary scholar in traditional Chinese thought, their graceful movements and dignified bearing appealing to a sense of propriety. Other emblems used as scholarly attributes were the lute (zin) for its ethereal music, the plum tree for the exquisite beauty of its blossoms, the pine tree for its strength and antiquity and the sword for the uprightness of the superior man. The flight and call of the crane inspired many tunes for the lute which are still played today although composed hundreds of years ago in the Sung and Ming dynasties. One such tune in three parts has these descriptive titles:

Ascending in the clouds with the crane as vehicle;
Riding on the wind up to the confines of heaven;
Treading the emptiness of the highest atmosphere.

Lutes were very beautiful hand-carved instruments and were highly prized by their owners. Individual lutes were traditionally given names and referred to by them. Lists of suitable names were compiled and among them are 'Friends of the Crane' (He you) and 'A Crane crying in the High Air' (Ling xiao he li).

Although the crane in its wild state is very wary of humans, there are many stories of cranes in captivity which become the inseparable companions of men and of cranes from the wild showing human understanding as in the Chinese story, The Crane Maiden. *Japan also has many legends about cranes, wounded or trapped in the wild, but then saved by kindly peasants. The crane in gratitude changes itself into a beautiful young woman and goes to live either as wife or daughter with her rescuer as in* The Crane Wife.

One of the most popular ways in Japan of using the crane as a symbol of happiness and peace is in the art of folding paper into bird, animal or other forms. From Japan the art of paper folding, origami, has become popular in western countries and there are many books showing how to fold paper into different patterns; see The World of Origami *by Isao Honda listed in* Further Reading. *Nearly two hundred years ago a book was written called* Sembazuru Orikata (Folding a Thousand Cranes). *Ever since Japanese children have strung up chains of a thousand paper cranes they have folded to make their wishes come true and their handiwork has taken on a religious significance. When praying for the outlawing of nuclear weapons, for example, thousands and thousands of paper cranes have been strung up as a prayer for peace.*

Note: Translations in this Introduction *are taken from* The Lore of the Chinese Lute *by R. H. van Gulik. Tokyo, 1940 (Tuttle, 1969).*

The Crane Maiden Story

Once upon a time there was a man called Tien Kun-lun. He was very poor, and was not able to marry a wife. In the land he owned there was a pond which was deep, clear and beautiful. Once when the crops were ripe he went to his field and saw that there were three beautiful girls washing themselves and bathing in the pond. Wanting to have a closer look at them he watched them from a hundred paces away. Two of them at once changed into white cranes, and flew away, but the third stayed in the pond, washing herself.

Tien Kun-lun pressed low down between the cornstalks and crept forward to look at her. These beautiful girls were heavenly maidens. The older ones clasped their heavenly robes and rode off into the sky, but the youngest, who was in the pond, did not dare come out. She made no secret of this, saying to Kun-lun: "We three sisters, who are Heavenly Maidens, came out to amuse ourselves for a while in this pond. But you, the owner of the pond, saw us. My two elder sisters were able to rescue their heavenly robes in time and escape. But I, the youngest, lingered all alone in the pond and you have taken away my heavenly robe and I cannot come naked out of the pond. Please do me the kindness to give it back to me, that I may cover my nakedness and come out of the pond. If you do so, I will marry you." But Kun-lun debated the matter in his mind and decided that if he gave her the heavenly robe, there was a danger that she might fly away. So he answered: "Madam, it is no use your asking for your heavenly robe, for you will never get it. But how would it be if I were to take off my shirt, so that for the time being you could cover yourself with that?"

At first the Heavenly Maiden refused to come out on these terms, and Kun-lun at last declared that it was getting dark and he must go. She tried to detain him, still asking for her robe, but when she found she could not get it, her tone changed and she said to Kun-lun, "Very well then! Give me your shirt to cover me while I come out of the pond, and I will marry you." Kun-lun was delighted. He rolled up the heavenly robe and hid it away. Then he took off his shirt and gave it to the Heavenly Maiden, to cover her when she came out of the pond. She said to Kun-lun, "Do not be afraid I shall go away. Let me put on my heavenly robe again, and I will go along with you." But Kun-lun would rather have died than give it to her, and without more ado he took her home with him to show her to his mother. The mother was delighted and ordered mats to be set out. All the friends and relatives of the family were invited and on the appointed day the girl was hailed as New Bride. Although she was a Heavenly Maiden, they lived together as man and wife. Days went and months came, and presently she bore him a son, a fine child, whom they named Tien Qang.

Soon afterwards Kun-lun was marked down for service in the west, and was away a long time. The Heavenly Maiden said to herself, "It is three years since my husband went away and I have been bringing up this child." Then she said to her mother-in-law, "I am a Heavenly Maiden. At the time I came, when I was small and young, my father made for me a heavenly robe, and with it I rode through the sky and came here. If I were to see that robe now, I wonder what size it would be. Let me have a look at it; I would dearly love to see it!"

Now on the day that Kun-lun went away, he had given strict orders to his mother, saying, "This is the Heavenly Maiden's robe. Keep it hidden away and do not let her see it. For if she sees it, she will certainly ride away with it through the sky, and will never be seen again." So they hid it away, and Kun-lun went off to the west.

After he went away, the Heavenly Maiden thought constantly about the robe, fretting about it all the time and never knowing a moment's happiness. She said to her mother-in-law, "Do let me just have a look at the heavenly robe!" She kept on worrying her about this, and at last her mother-in-law decided to fall in with her wish. So she told her daughter-in-law to go outside the gate for a little while and then quietly come back. She went out at once and the mother-in-law took out the heavenly robe from its hiding place and when the Heavenly Maiden came back, showed it to her. When she saw it, her heart was cut to the quick, her tears fell like floods of rain, and she longed to ride off through the air. But having thought out no plan to do this, she had to give the robe back to her mother-in-law, who again hid it away.

Less than ten days later she said once more to her mother-in-law, "Let me have another look at my heavenly robe." The mother-in-law said, "I was afraid you might put it on, and fly away from us."

The daughter-in-law said, "I was once a Heavenly Maiden. But now I am married to your son and we have a child. How can you think I would leave you? Such a thing is impossible." The mother-in-law gave in, but was still afraid that she might fly away, and set someone to keep strict watch at the main gate.

But the Heavenly Maiden, as soon as she had put on the robe, flew straight up into the sky through the roof vent. The old woman beat her breast and in great distress hurried out of the door to see what happened to her. She arrived in time to see her soaring away into the sky. The mother-in-law, when she knew that she had lost her daughter-in-law, let out such a cry as pierced the bright sky; her tears fell like rain, she became utterly desperate and in the bitter sorrow of her heart all day she would not eat.

The Heavenly Maiden had passed more than five years in the world of men, and now she had spent her first two days in heaven above. When she escaped and reached her home both her sisters cursed her for a shameless baggage. "By marrying that common creature of the world of men," they said, "you have made your father and mother so sad they do nothing but weep." "However," they said, "it is no good your continually lamenting for your son as you are doing now. Tomorrow we three sisters will go together and play at the pool. Then you will certainly see your child again."

The child Tien Qang had just reached his fifth year. At that time there was a certain Master Tung Zhung who was always seeking for persons of superior conduct. He knew that this was the child of a Heavenly Maiden and knew that the Heavenly Maiden was about to come down to the lower world. So he said to the child, "Just at midday go to the side of the pond and look. Three women will come all dressed in white silk robes. Two of them will raise their heads and look at you; but one will lower her head and pretend not to see you, and that one will be your mother."

Tien Qang did as Tung Zhung told him, and just at midday he saw beside the pond three Heavenly Maidens, all dressed in white silk robes, cutting salad-herbs at the edge of the pond. Tien Qang went nearer and looked at them. Seeing him from afar they knew that it was the child who had come, and the two elder sisters said to the younger, "Your child has come." Then he called out to his mother. But she, although she hung her head in shame and did not look at him, could not stop her sorrow from coming out of her heart, and she wept bitterly. The three sisters then took their heavenly robes and carried the child away with them into the sky.

Abbreviated from *Ballads and Stories from Tun-huang: an Anthology* by Arthur Waley. Used by courtesy of the publisher, George Allen & Unwin Ltd. London ©1960.

Tun-huang in the far north-west of China is the site of the Caves of the Thousand Buddhas carved into the living rock. In 1900 a Taoist monk, while restoring one of the many fresco paintings on the stone walls of the caves found that the underneath surface was brick not stone. Carefully removing one brick he peered in and discovered a smaller cave piled high with rolls of manuscripts. The cave had been bricked up some nine hundred years earlier to protect the monastery library from invaders. The manuscripts date from the fourth to the tenth centuries AD. Most are Buddhist texts but some eighty pieces of popular literature were found and among them *The Crane Maiden* story.

The Crane Wife

Once there was a man named Karoku. He lived with his seventy-year-old mother far back in the mountains, where he made charcoal for a living. One winter, as he was going to the village to buy some futon (bedding), he saw a crane struggling in a trap where it had been caught. Just as Karoku was stooping to release the poor crane, the man who had set the trap came running up.

"What are you doing, interfering with other people's business?" he cried.

"I felt so sorry for the crane I thought I would let it go. Will you sell it to me? Here, I have the money I was going to use to buy futon. Please take the money, and let me have the crane."

The man agreed, and Karoku took the crane and immediately let it fly away free.

"We may get cold tonight," thought Karoku, returning home, "but it can't be helped." When he got home, his mother asked what he had done with the futon. He replied, "I saw a crane caught in a trap. I felt so sorry for it that I used all the money to buy it and set it free."

"Well," his mother said, "since you have done it, I suppose that it is all right."

The next evening, just as night was falling, a beautiful young woman such as he had never seen before came to Karoku's house. "Please let me spend the night here," she asked, but Karoku refused, saying, "My little hut is too poor." She replied, "No, I do not mind; please, I implore you, let me stay," until finally he consented, and she was allowed to spend the night. During the evening she said, "I have something I should like to discuss with you," and when Karoku asked what it was, she replied, "I beg of you, please make me your wife."

Karoku, greatly surprised, said: "This is the first time in my life that I have seen such a beautiful woman as you. I am a very poor man; I do not even know where my next meal is coming from; how could I ever take you as my wife?"

Please do not refuse," she pleaded; "please take me as your wife."

"Well, as you beg me so much, I don't know what to do," he

replied. When his mother heard of this, she said to the woman, "Since you insist, you may become my son's bride. Please stay here and work hard." Soon preparations were made, and they were married.

Some time after this Karoku's wife said, "Please let me go into the weaving room and leave me there for three days. Close the door tightly and be sure not to open it to look at me." Her husband shut her into the weaving room, and on the fourth day, she came out. "It must have been very unpleasant in there," he said. "I was worried about you. Hurry and have something to eat."

After she finished eating she said, "Karoku, please take this cloth that I have woven and sell it for two thousand ryo." So saying, she gave the piece of cloth to her husband. He took it to the lord of the province, who, when he saw it, said, "This is very beautiful material, I will pay you two or even three thousand ryo for it. Can you bring me another piece like it?"

"I must ask my wife if she can weave another," Karoku replied.

"Oh, you need not ask her; it is all right if only you agree. I will give you the money for it now," the lord said.

Karoku returned home and told his wife what the lord had said.

"Just give me time and I'll weave another piece, she said. "This time please shut me in the room for one week. During that time you must be sure not to open the door and look at me."

By the time the week was nearly over, Karoku became very worried about his wife. On the last day of the week, he opened the door to see if she were all right. There inside the room was a crane, naked after having pulled out all her beautiful long feathers. She was using her feathers to weave the cloth and was just at the point of finishing it. The crane cried out, "I have finished the cloth, but since you have seen who I really am, I am afraid that you can no longer love me. I must return to my home. I am not a person but the crane whom you rescued. Please take the cloth to the lord as you promised. After she had said this, the crane silently turned toward the west. When she did this, thousands of cranes appeared and, taking her with them, they all flew out of sight.

Karoku had become a rich man, but he wanted to see his beloved wife so badly that he could not bear it. He searched for her throughout Japan until he was exhausted. One day as he was sitting on the seashore resting, he saw an old man alone in a rowing boat, approaching from the open ocean. "How strange," thought Karoku. "Where could he be coming from; there are no islands near here." As he sat in bewilderment, the boat landed on the beach. Karoku called out, "Grandfather, where did you come from?"

"I came from an island called 'The Robe of Crane Feathers'," the old man replied.

Would you please take me to that island?" asked Karoku.

The man quickly agreed, and Karoku climbed into the boat. The boat sped over the water, and in no time they had arrived at a beautiful white beach. They landed, and when Karoku got out of the boat and turned around, the boat and the old man had vanished from sight.

Karoku walked up the beach and soon came to a beautiful lake. In the middle of the lake was an island, and there on the island was the naked crane. She was surrounded by a myriad of cranes, for she was queen of the cranes. Karoku stayed a short while and was given a feast. Afterwards the old man with the boat returned, and Karoku was taken back to his home.

From *Folk Tales of Japan*. Edited by Keigo Seki. Translated by Robert J. Adams. (Folktales of the World.)

The story as told here is taken from two hundred and forty most representative folk tales selected by Keigo Seki from the more than fifteen thousand collected from oral tradition by scholarly Japanese folklorists during the twentieth century. It has been made into a popular drama in Japan by Junjiro Kinoshita and translated into English by A. C. Scott in *Playbook; a New Directions Book*, New York, 1956.

Poems from Classical Chinese and Japanese and A True Chinese Story

Perhaps the oldest extant poem in the world about a crane is the first of the four following Chinese poems. It is traditionally supposed to have been among those collected by the sage-philosopher Confucius, in the sixth century BC. This poem and the next one by Du Mu who lived in the ninth century AD offer homage to the wild crane, while the other two Chinese poems, also from the ninth century AD, concern the relationship between cranes and men.

All four of the Japanese poems are taken from the Manyoshu, *a collection of one thousand poems written between the fifth and eighth centuries AD. It is the oldest anthology of Japanese poetry and was first collected about the time of the later eighth century poems. The translations are the work of the Classics Translation Committee of the Nippon Gakujutsu Shinkokai, a cultural and scientific society founded in 1932. The first two poems link the melancholy cry of cranes with loneliness in the human heart, while the last two show the association of cranes with the beauties of nature.*

A true story ends this anthology. It is again from ninth century China and is retold from a guide book to the West Lake in Hangchow bought there in 1956 by the present compiler-editor. Other more recent guide books to the West Lake publish the same story.

The Cry of a Crane

The crane cries in the Nine Marshes,
Its voice carries into the wilds;
The fish plunges into the deep, or lies by the islet;
Pleasant is that garden,
It is planted with tan trees,
Under them are fallen leaves.
. . .

The crane cries in the Nine Marshes,
Its voice carries up to heaven;
The fish lies by the islet, or . . . plunges into the deep;
Pleasant is that garden,
It is planted with tan trees,
Under them are fallen leaves.
. . .

From *The Book of Odes.* Chinese text, transcription and translation by Bernhard Kalgren. (A two-line chorus with doubtful meaning has been omitted.)

The Cranes

[AD 830]

The western wind has blown but a few days;
Yet the first leaf already flies from the bough.
On the drying paths I walk in my thin shoes;
In the first cold I have donned my quilted coat.
Through shallow ditches the floods are clearing away;
Through sparse bamboos trickles a slanting light.
In the early dusk, down an alley of green moss,
The garden-boy is leading the cranes home.

By Bo Ju-yi (AD 772-846).
Translated by Arthur Waley.

From *Chinese Poems* by Arthur Waley, 1946.

Used by courtesy of the publisher, George Allen & Unwin Ltd., London.

The Crane

With a pure note he welcomes the evening moon,
With sad thoughts he stands on cold bulrush.
Red head and cheeks like Hsi Shih's;
Frosty feathers and beard all white like the Four
Venerable Old Men's.
Beneath jasper clouds, moving and stopping restlessly;
To him the spirit of the white egret is coarse.
All day long without the companionship of a flock,
By the side of the gully he laments his shadow's
solitude.

By Du Mu (AD 803-852).
Translated by John M. Ortineau.

From *Sunflower Splendor: Three Thousand Years of Chinese Poetry.* Co-edited by Wu-chi Liu and Irving Yucheng Lo.

Remembering the Crane I Released

Living in retirement at Wu-hsi
A villager gave me a fledgling crane.
A year later, its feathers grown,
Pitying its yearning to fly,
I released it from its cage.
It soared into the sky
Circling round and round
Before finally leaving me.

Its feathers white as unsullied snow
It gazed at its own reflection
And danced with the white clouds
Mirrored in the Autumn pond
Like a celestial being from the fairy isles.
The lingering echo of its ringing cry resounded
in the skies.

It soared with the wind and seemed to brush past
the sun.
'Do not regret leaving me! Your destiny is to reach
heaven!'
I sat and watched it disappear into the blue
Pitying the herons and the loons which must grow
old by the river bank.

By Li Shen (died AD 845).

From *The Complete Poems of the Tang Dynasty* (Chinese text) translated by Tsai-fa Cheng and Dorothea Hayward Scott.

The four poems which follow are taken from *The Manyoshu: One Thousand Poems,* selected and translated from the Japanese. Tokyo, 1940. Published for the Nippon Gakujutsu Shinkokai by the Iwanami Shoten.

The mallards call with evening from the reeds
And float with dawn midway on the water;
They sleep with their mates it is said,
With white wings overlapping and tails a-sweep
Lest the frost should fall upon them.

As the stream that flows never returns,
And as the wind that blows is never seen,
My wife of this world has left me,
Gone I know not whither!
So here, on the sleeves of these clothes
She used to have me wear,
I sleep now all alone!

Cranes call flying to the reedy shore,
How desolate I remain
As I sleep alone!

Tajihi —
(Nara period AD 710-784)

On an evening when the spring mists
Trail over the wide sea,
And sad is the voice of the cranes
I think of my far-off home.

Thinking of home,
Sleepless I sit,
The cranes call amid the shore reeds,
Lost in the mists of spring.

Otomo Yakamoshi (AD 718-785)

Climbing the Hill of Kami

Continuously, as their name tells,
The tsuga trees that grow in luxuriance
With five hundred boughs outbranching,
On Mount Kamunabi of Mimoro —
And as endlessly as the creeping vine,
I would visit these ruins
Of the Palace of Asuka.
Here the hill is high, the river long;
On a spring day the hill is sweetest,
The stream is limpid of an autumn night,
The cranes wing the morning clouds in flocks,
The frogs call in the evening mists;
Whenever I gaze upon them
I am bowed in tears
Remembering the days of old.

Yamabe Akahito
(Early – middle Nara period AD 710-784).

Shall I not miss the dainty seaweed
On the rugged island beach
When it is hidden under the flood tide?

As the tide flows into Waka Bay,
The cranes, with the lagoons lost in flood,
Go crying towards the reedy shore.

Yamabe Akahito
(Early – middle Nara period AD 710-784).

Flying Crane Pavilion

Over seven hundred years ago when Marco Polo travelled to China, he described Hangzou with its beautiful West Lake as without doubt the finest and most splendid city in the world. The West Lake is surrounded by mountains on which there are numerous temples and pagodas. Across a section of the Lake there is a handsome causeway with carved stone balustrades and small pavilions. The causeway joins the tip of a peninsula to the mainland forming an inner lake with waters which are always calm. On this peninsula there is a high hill known as Lonely Hill because in early times it was far from the city.

Towards the end of the tenth century AD, a poet-painter who wished to retire from the world and devote himself to his art, built himself a hut on Lonely Hill where he lived and worked. His name was Lin He-Qing. His only companion besides a servant-cook was a crane which he had reared himself. It was very tame. When Lin was not painting or composing poetry he spent his time making a beautiful garden around his hut. He planted more than three hundred plum trees. The blossom in springtime was a sight to be seen. So happy was Lin with his crane and his plum trees that people said he had the plum trees for his wife and the crane for a son. If he was away from home when visitors came the servant would call the crane to stay with the guest until his master returned. When the master came back and was sitting drinking tea or wine with his visitor and reciting his latest poems, the crane would spread its great wings and fly around overhead to add to the entertainment.

When Lin eventually died he was buried on Lonely Hill and his tomb can be seen there today. The crane died too, it was said it died of sorrow, and all the plum trees withered. The crane lies buried in a tomb near its master's. A hundred years after Lin's death a temple and a pavilion were built near his tomb to commemorate him. The temple no longer exists but the pavilion has been restored and a fine terrace has been built where his hut stood and hundreds of plum trees have been planted. It is called the Flying Crane Pavilion (Fang He Ting).

Retold by the editor from a 1956 guide book to the West Lake at Hangchow printed in Beijing by the Foreign Languages Press. Other recent West Lake guide books publish the same story.

Red-crowned Crane

Cranes of the World

Whooping Crane

The following description of the cranes of the world has been condensed from an account prepared by the Education Department of the International Crane Foundation, a leading scientific organization located in Wisconsin, USA, and with the mission of saving cranes everywhere. It was founded in 1972 by George Archibald and Ron Sauey, two scientists who have dedicated their lives to this cause. The aims of the Foundation are:

1. *RESEARCH at home and abroad, to learn more about cranes and to find solutions to problems they face.*
2. *HABITAT PRESERVATION programs, to encourage the wise conservation of habitats essential to cranes and other organisms.*
3. *CAPTIVE PROPAGATION to build viable populations of each of the endangered species, in cooperation with other breeding centres. These birds will comprise a 'species bank' for study and propagation.*
4. *RESTOCKING PROGRAM designed to return eggs and/or young birds to their native habitats when conditions are safe and appropriate.*
5. *PUBLIC EDUCATION to inform the public and involve people in the goals of the Foundation and conservation in general.*

The Foundation now has fine premises of 160 acres in Baraboo, Wisconsin. The facility has special units for housing, propagating and maintaining cranes from day old chicks to adult breeding pairs. In the Schroeder Exhibit Room visitors of all ages can study the intricacies of bird reproduction.

Other countries, often inspired and helped by the International Crane Foundation, are working to save their cranes. Japan, China, North and South Korea, Vietnam, India, U.S.S.R., Kenya, Nigeria and dozens of other countries all have dedicated scientists working with different wild life organizations to this end.

Cranes of the World

Cranes have been around for sixty million years and may have shared this planet with dinosaurs. The sandhill crane of North America is the oldest living species of bird and has been virtually unchanged for nine million years. Cranes are found on all continents of the world except South America and Antarctica. Most cranes prefer wetlands and place the nest in a location where it will be surrounded by water, if possible. The destruction of the world's wetlands has been the major enemy of cranes, although hunting and pollution have taken their toll as well. Since cranes are large birds they require considerable space to raise their young, and this need has contributed to their plight. There are fifteen different species of cranes left in the world, and seven of these are endangered. The following information is designed to give a better understanding and greater appreciation of these magnificent birds.

Cranes are large birds closely related to coots and rails. They fly with neck outstretched and feet trailing — this habit helps to distinguish them from better known herons and egrets. Another distinguishing feature of most cranes is the red patch of bare skin on their head. The colour is brightest during the breeding season. Cranes have a short elevated hind toe and do not normally perch in trees. The wing feathers are so long that they cover the tail and give the appearance of a bustle. They are long-lived birds surviving more than thirty years in the wild. One captive bird lived for sixty-one years and another is unofficially reported to have lived for eighty-seven years in a zoo.

Cranes normally mate for life. Once a partner has been selected the pair will probably remain together for as long as both live. If one of the pair dies, however, the other will remate. As spring approaches both male and female intensify their courtship activities and defend a suitable nesting territory prior to egg laying. The pair must acquire enough habitat if they are to breed successfully. One especially interesting feature of a crane's life history is the elaborate courtship dance which pairs perform. The dance helps a pair synchronize its breeding readiness and may even be performed when the birds are disturbed or angry. The dance includes head bobbing, wing flapping, running and twig tossing and is fascinating to watch. Cranes have a special unison call which pairs perform to announce possession of territory or simply to assert themselves. This call is performed as a male/female duet; as both the posture and voice vary between the sexes, the call provides an easy way of distinguishing male from female since they look identical. Cranes are also noted for their loud bugling calls which can be heard up to two or three miles away.

Cranes usually lay just two eggs, but if a predator destroys the eggs during the early stages of nesting, the female may lay again. The eggs are incubated for twenty-eight to thirty-two days with both male and female sharing the incubation duties. Within hours of hatching the chicks leave the nest with their parents and forage where food is abundant. Crane chicks grow extremely fast — as much as four feet in three months for one species. They continue growing slowly for the next year or more and reach maturity at age three.

When the chicks are two and a half to three months old they are able to fly and begin strengthening their muscles for migration. Once cold weather begins, the crane family moves south to the wintering grounds. The young must learn the migration route from their parents as they travel. Many cranes migrate long distances between their summer and winter habitats, flying between two and three thousand miles every season. The families form loose flocks in staging areas where abundant food is available. These areas tend to be used from generation to generation and there may be hundreds or even thousands of birds resting at one time. Although the cold winter temperatures of the northern areas may seem to make migration necessary, it is actually the lack of food and water which forces many species to leave. Most cranes are cold-hardy and do not mind winter temperatures. During the winter months the family feeds and loafs before its return flight in the spring. Once the family has returned to the breeding grounds the young are no longer tolerated but are chased away from the nesting area as the parents begin preparing for the new season. The young cranes must now care for themselves and at this time often mingle with other unpaired birds in 'bachelor' flocks until they find a mate.

Cranes eat both plant and animal material. Their diet consists of a wide variety of foods and changes with the time of the year and feeding location. Crane chicks require considerably more protein (animal material) than the adults due to their enormous growth rate. They will eat fish, frogs, small rodents and reptiles, beetles and insects as well as grains. The long bill and legs make it possible for them to wade in water or through deep grasses in search of their food. When the chicks are small the parents capture most of their food and offer small bits to them, but they are left to forage on their own as soon as possible.

The names of the species of cranes in the world are given with the illustrations on the following two pages.

For the captive cranes at the International Crane Foundation conditions are simulated to be like those in the wild as far as possible. A pair establishes its territory, builds a nest together and eggs are laid. But as soon as this happens the egg is removed from the nest and artificially incubated or put with foster sandhill crane parents. In this way as many as eight eggs may be produced by a pair in a season. All the chicks are hand reared and great progress is now being made in successfully re-introducing young cranes into the wild under suitable conditions. In this way it is hoped to gradually re-establish endangered species in their natural habitats throughout the world, the main aim of the Foundation.

Cranes of the World

Red-crowned Crane

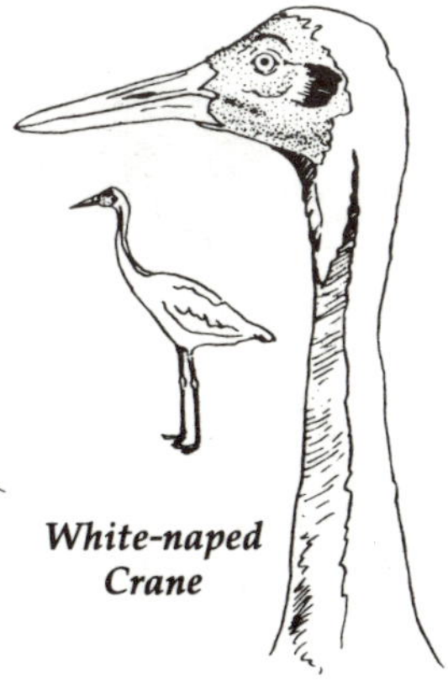

White-naped Crane

Wattled Crane

Siberian Crane

Endangered Species of Cranes

Hooded Crane

Whooping Crane

Black-necked Crane

Cranes of the World

Demoiselle Crane

Gray Crowned Crane

Brolga

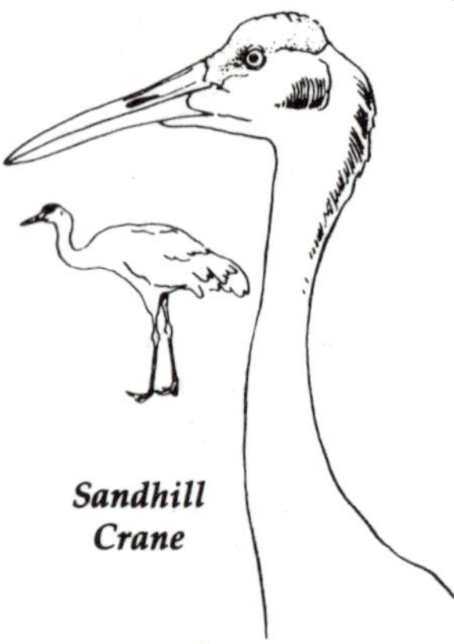

Sandhill Crane

Non-Endangered Species of Cranes

Sarus Crane

Common Crane

Stanley Crane

Black Crowned Crane

Further Reading

The Cranes. Compiled by J. C. Sawhuey. Published for the World Wildlife Fund – India by the compiler. Parel, Bombay, India 400012.

The Japanese Crane: Bird of Happiness. Dorothy Britton/Tsuneo Hayashida. Tokyo, New York, San Francisco, Kodansha International, 1981.

The Red-crowned Crane. Published by the China Pictorial Press, Beijing, 1983.

(Available from the International Crane Foundation, Baraboo, Wisconsin, 53913.)

The Whooping Crane: the Bird That Defies Extinction. By Faith McNulty. Toronto, Clark Irwin, 1966.

The World of Origami by Isao Honda. San Francisco, Japan Publications Trading Company, 1983 (1965).